THINGS MOTHER USED TO MAKE

A Collection of Old Time Recipes, Some Nearly One
Hundred Years Old and Never Published Before.

By LYDIA MARIA GURNEY

Originally published in 1914.

AUTHOR'S FOREWORD

Good food depends as largely upon the judgment of the cook, as upon the materials used. These recipes and Household Hints are written very plainly, for those who have had no experience, no practice and possibly have little judgment.

They are very simple, not expensive, and if followed closely, will ensure success. It is the hope of the writer of this book that the young and inexperienced housekeeper may find it a real help.

L.M. GURNEY

INTRODUCTION

The Things Mother Used To Make consist of old fashioned recipes, which have been for the most part handed down by word of mouth from one generation to another, extending over a period of nearly one hundred years. The author, a New England woman, has during her life tested out in her own kitchen the greater part of these recipes, which represent the best cookery of those times.

This material was originally published in Suburban Life, where it obtained such recognition as seemed to warrant its preservation in book form. The original material has accordingly been amplified, and it is here presented as one of the volumes in the series of Countryside Manuals.

FRANK A. ARNOLD

NEW YORK

September 15, 1913

BREADS

Bannocks

1 Cupful of Thick Sour Milk 1/2 Cupful of Sugar 1 Egg 2 Cupfuls of Flour 1/2 Cupful of Indian Meal 1 Teaspoonful of Soda A pinch of Salt

Make the mixture stiff enough to drop from a spoon. Drop mixture, size of a walnut, into boiling fat. Serve warm, with maple syrup.

Boston Brown Bread

1 Cupful of Rye Meal 1 Cupful of Graham Meal 1 Cupful of Indian Meal 1 Cupful of Sweet Milk 1 Cupful of Sour Milk 1 Cupful of Molasses 1 Teaspoonful of Salt 1 Heaping Teaspoonful of Soda

Stir the meals and salt together. Beat the soda into the molasses until it foams; add sour milk, mix all together and pour into a tin pail which has been well greased, if you have no brown-bread steamer.

Set the pail into a kettle of boiling water and steam three or four hours, keeping it tightly covered.

Brown Bread (Baked)

1 Cupful of Indian Meal 1 Cupful of Rye Meal 1/2 Cupful of Flour 1 Cupful of Molasses (scant) 1 Cupful of Milk or Water 1 Teaspoonful of Soda

Put the meals and flour together. Stir soda into molasses until it foams. Add salt and milk or water.

Mix all together. Bake in a tin pail with cover on for two and a half hours.

Coffee Cakes

When your dough for yeast bread is risen light and fluffy, cut off small pieces and roll as big as your finger, four inches long. Fold and twist to two inches long and fry in deep fat. Serve hot with coffee.

Corn Meal Gems

2 Cupfuls of Flour 1 Cupful of Corn Meal (bolted is best) 2 Cupfuls of Milk 2 Teaspoonfuls of Cream of Tartar 1 Teaspoonful of Baking Soda 1 Egg 1/2 Cupful of Sugar 1/2 Teaspoonful of Salt

Stir the flour and meal together, adding cream of tartar, soda, salt and sugar. Beat the egg, add the milk to it, and stir into the other ingredients. Bake in a gem-pan twenty minutes.

Cream of Tartar Biscuits

1 Pint of Flour 2 Teaspoonfuls of Cream of Tartar 1 Teaspoonful of Soda 1/2 Teaspoonful of Salt 1 Tablespoonful of Lard

Stir cream of tartar, soda, salt and lard into the flour; mix with milk or water, handling as little as possible. Roll and cut into rounds. Baking-powder can be used in place of soda and cream of tartar.

Crullers

Use the recipe for doughnuts, adding one egg and a little more butter. Roll a small piece of the dough to the size of your finger, and eight inches long, double it, and twist the two rolls together. Fry in boiling fat.

Delicious Dip Toast

Cut slices of bread, one-half inch thick; toast each side to a delicate brown. Dip these into hot, salted milk, letting them remain until soft. Lay them on a platter and spread a little butter over each slice.

Take one quart of milk more or less according to size of family; heat in a double boiler, salt to taste. Wet two tablespoonfuls of flour with a little water; stir until smooth, and pour into the milk when boiling. Make this of the consistency of rich cream; add a piece of butter the size of a walnut, and pour over the toasted bread. Serve hot.

Doughnuts

1 Egg 1 Cupful of Milk 1 and 1/3 Cupfuls of Sugar 2 Teaspoonfuls of Cream of Tartar 1 Teaspoonful of Soda Piece of Butter the Size of a Walnut 1/4 Teaspoonful of Cinnamon or Nutmeg Salt, and Flour enough to roll soft

Beat the egg and sugar together and add the milk and butter. Stir the soda and cream of tartar into the flour, dry; mix all together, with the flour and salt. Cut into rings and fry in deep fat. Lay them on brown paper when you take them from the fat.

Fried Bread

After frying pork or bacon, put into the fat slices of stale bread. As it fries, pour over each slice a little milk or water and salt to taste, turn and fry on the opposite side. This is a very appetizing dish.

German Toast

1 Cupful of Milk 1 Egg Pinch of Salt 4 or 5 Slices of Bread

Beat together one egg, one cupful of milk, and a little salt. Dip slices of stale bread into this mixture, and fry on a griddle in butter or pork fat. Serve hot with butter and maple syrup.

Soft Gingerbread

1 Cupful of Molasses 1 Cupful of Sour Milk 1/2 Cupful of Butter or Lard 1 Teaspoonful of Ginger 1 Teaspoonful of Soda 1/2 Teaspoonful of Salt

Stir the soda into the molasses until it foams, add sour milk, ginger, salt and melted butter. Last of all, add flour enough for quite a stiff batter, and bake. This makes one sheet.

Huckleberry Cake

Pick over and wash and flour well one cupful of fresh huckleberries.

Add these to the batter for soft gingerbread. Serve hot, with butter.

Quick Graham Bread

1 Pint of Graham Meal 1/2 Cupful of Molasses 1 Cupful of Sour Milk 1 Teaspoonful of Soda 1 Teaspoonful of Salt

Stir soda into the molasses, add sour milk and salt; add all to the meal, beating well. Sweet milk will do with a little less soda. Bake thirty minutes, or according to heat of the oven. A moderate oven is best.

Graham Bread (raised over night)

3 Cupfuls of Flour 3 Cupfuls of Graham Meal 3 Tablespoonfuls of Sugar 1 Tablespoonful of Lard 1 Teaspoonful of Salt 1 Yeast Cake

Mix flour and meal together and rub in lard, sugar and salt. Add yeast cake which has been dissolved in one-half cup of cold water. Mix with warm water at night. Set in a warm place to rise. In the morning stir and let rise to twice its bulk. Knead and put in baking pans. Raise again and bake forty-five minutes.

Graham Muffins

1 Pint of Graham Flour 1/2 Cupful of Molasses 1 Teaspoonful of Salt 1/2 Pint of White Flour 1 Teaspoonful of Soda

Put the salt into the flour and soda into the molasses. Stir all together and mix with milk or water. Drop into muffin tins and bake twenty minutes.

Sour Milk Griddle Cakes

2 Cupfuls of Sour Milk 2 Teaspoonfuls of Soda 1 Teaspoonful of Salt

Stir the soda and salt into the milk and add flour enough to make thin batter. Fry on a well-greased griddle. One spoonful for each cake. Serve hot with butter and maple syrup.

Sweet Milk Griddle Cakes

1 Egg 1 Pint of Sweet Milk 2 Level Teaspoonfuls of Cream of Tartar 1 Level Teaspoonful of Soda Pinch of Salt Flour enough for thin batter

Mix soda and cream of tartar with flour. Beat the egg, add milk and stir into flour. Fry in small cakes on a griddle.

Jenny Lind Tea Cake

3 Cupfuls of Flour 1/2 Cupful of Sugar 1 Egg 1 Teaspoonful of Soda 1 Tablespoonful of Melted Butter 2 Teaspoonfuls of Cream of Tartar

Stir salt, soda and cream of tartar into the dry flour. Beat the egg, add sugar and butter, stir into the flour and mix with enough milk to make batter as thick as a cake. Bake in a moderate oven. To be eaten hot with butter.

Real Johnny Cake

2 Cupfuls of Flour 1 Cupful of Yellow Meal 4 Tablespoonfuls of Sugar 1 Teaspoonful of Salt 1 Teaspoonful of Cream of Tartar 1/2 Teaspoonful of Soda or 2 Teaspoonfuls of Baking-powder

Add enough milk or water to make a thin batter, and bake.

New England Buns

1 Cupful of Milk 1 and l/3 Cupfuls of Sugar 2/3 Cupful of Butter or Lard 1/2 Cupful of Currants 1 Teaspoonful of Extract of Lemon 1/4 Teaspoonful of Soda 1/2 Teaspoonful of Salt 1 Yeast Cake Flour enough for Soft Dough

Dissolve the yeast in a half-cupful of cold water. Scald the milk and, when nearly cold, add the yeast, half the sugar, and flour enough to make a thin batter; let it rise to twice its bulk. When light and foamy, add the rest of the ingredients; sprinkle a little flour over the currants, stir the soda into the flour, using flour enough to make stiff dough. Set again, then roll, cut with a cooky-cutter, about an inch thick, and let rise again. Bake in a moderate oven twenty-five minutes. Mix in the morning, if wanted for the evening meal. When done, brush over the top, while warm, with equal parts of milk and molasses.

Nut Bread

2 1/2 Cupfuls of Flour 3 Teaspoonfuls of Baking-powder 1/4 Teaspoonful of Salt 1/2 Cupful of Sugar 1 Egg 1 Cupful of Milk 3/4 Cupful of English Walnut Meats, chopped fine

Beat egg and sugar together, then add milk and salt. Sift the baking-powder into the dry flour, and put all the ingredients together. Add the nuts last, covering with a little flour, to prevent falling, and bake in a moderate oven one hour.

Oatmeal Bread

2 Cupfuls of Rolled Oats 3 1/2 Cupfuls of Boiling Water 1/2 Cupful of Molasses 1 Yeast Cake Pinch of Salt

Let the rolled oats and boiling water stand until cool, then add the molasses, salt, and yeast cake which has been dissolved in cold water. Stir in flour enough to make a stiff dough. Let it rise over night. In the morning, stir it down and let it rise again. Mold into loaves and let rise again.

Bake forty-five minutes in a moderate oven.

This will make three small loaves.

Parker House Rolls

1 Quart of Flour 1 Tablespoonful of Lard 3 Tablespoonfuls of Sugar 1 Teaspoonful of Salt 1/2 Pint of Milk 1 Yeast Cake

Scald the milk. When nearly cold add the yeast cake which has been dissolved in one-half cup of cold water. Rub into the flour, the lard, sugar and salt. Stir all together with a knife and knead. Let rise to twice its bulk and knead. Let rise again and knead. Roll half an inch thick, cut into rounds, spread with butter and double over. Rise again, bake twenty minutes in a hot oven. Mix at ten o'clock in the morning if wanted for supper, a little earlier in cold weather.

Popovers

1 Egg 1 Cupful of Milk 1 Cupful of Flour

Beat the egg, and stir flour and milk in slowly, a little flour, then a little milk. Salt a little. This will make a very thin batter. Drop into well-buttered muffin pan, bake in a very hot oven and serve with hot sauce for a pudding, or eat with butter.

Rye Muffins

2 Cupfuls of Flour 1 Cupful of Rye Meal 3 Tablespoonfuls of Sugar 1 Teaspoonful of Salt 1/3 Cupful of Yeast or 1 Yeast Cake dissolved in Water

Mix with warm water at night. In the morning add one-quarter teaspoonful of soda, dissolved in two tablespoonfuls of boiling water; stir well. Bake in a gem-pan for twenty or thirty minutes.

Breakfast Sally Lunn

1 Egg 1 Quart of Flour Piece of Butter the size of an Egg 4 Tablespoonfuls of Sugar 2 Teacupfuls of Milk 2

Teaspoonfuls of Cream of Tartar 1 Teaspoonful of Soda A little Salt

Mix salt, sugar, cream of tartar and soda, with the flour. Beat the egg, stir into it the melted butter and milk. Stir all together and bake in a muffin pan, fifteen or twenty minutes.

Sour Milk Biscuits

1 Pint of Flour 1 Teaspoonful of Lard 1 Teaspoonful of Soda 1 Teaspoonful of Salt 1 Cupful of Sour Milk

Put lard and salt into the flour and soda with the sour milk. Mix together, roll thin and cut into rounds. Bake twenty minutes.

Spider Cake

2 Cupfuls of Bread Flour 1/3 Cupful of Lard 2 Teaspoonfuls of Cream of Tartar 1 Teaspoonful of Soda 1 Teaspoonful of Salt

Put the soda, salt and cream of tartar into the dry flour. Rub in the lard and mix with water into a soft dough. Roll to the size of the spider or griddle. When the spider is hot and well greased with lard, lay on the cake and cover. Bake ten minutes on one side, then ten on the other. This can be made quickly without waiting for the oven to heat. Serve hot with butter.

White Bread

3 Cupfuls of Flour 3 Teaspoonfuls of Sugar 1 Teaspoonful of Lard 1 Pinch of Salt 1/2 Yeast Cake

Rub sugar, salt and lard into the flour. Dissolve the yeast in half a cupful of cold water. Put all together and mix to a stiff dough with milk or water, at night. In the morning, push it down and let rise again. Then knead and place in a pan. Let it rise to twice its bulk and bake thirty minutes.

CAKES

Filled Cookies

1 Cupful of Sugar 1/2 Cupful of Butter or Lard 1 Cupful of Milk 3 1/2 Cupfuls of Flour 2 Teaspoonfuls of Cream of Tartar 1 Teaspoonful of Soda 1 Tablespoonful of Vanilla

Roll thin and cut with a cooky-cutter.

Filling for Cookies

1 Cupful of Chopped Raisins 1/2 Cupful of Sugar 1/2 Cupful of Water 1 Teaspoonful of Flour

Cook this until thick, being careful not to burn it. Place cookies in a well-buttered pan, spread on a teaspoonful of the filling and cover with another cooky. Bake in a moderate oven.

Sugar Cookies

1 Cupful of Sugar 1/2 Cupful of Butter 2 Tablespoonfuls of Milk 1 Egg 2 Teaspoonfuls of Cream of Tartar 1 Teaspoonful of Soda 1 Teaspoonful of Lemon Extract Flour enough to roll

Beat the butter, sugar and egg together, add the milk, stir the cream of tartar and soda into the flour dry. Stir all together and roll.

Cream Cake

2 Eggs 1 Cupful of Cream (sour preferred) 1 Cupful of
Sugar 2 Cupfuls of Flour 1 Teaspoonful of Soda 1/2
Teaspoonful of Salt Flavor with Lemon

Stir the soda into the cream; beat the eggs; add sugar, salt,
flour and cream; last of all, the flavoring.

Delicious Cake without Eggs

1 Cupful of Thick, Sour Milk 1 Cupful of Sugar 1/2 Cupful
of Butter 2 Cupfuls of Flour 1 Cupful of Chopped Raisins
Pinch of Salt 1 Teaspoonful of Soda 1 Teaspoonful of
Cinnamon 1/2 Teaspoonful each of Cloves and Nutmeg

Stir the soda into the sour milk, add melted butter and
sugar, salt and spices. Put the flour over the raisins and stir
all together. This will make one loaf or twelve little cakes
in gem-pans.

Feather Cake

2 Cupfuls of Sugar 3 Eggs Butter the size of an Egg 1
Teaspoonful of Cream of Tartar 1/2 Teaspoonful of Soda 3
Cupfuls of Flour Flavor with Almond Beat fifteen minutes

Cream together the butter and sugar. Add the well-beaten
eggs, then the milk. Beat together. Put soda and cream of
tartar into the flour, dry. Stir all together with the flavoring.
This will make two small loaves.

Old-time Gingersnaps

1 Cupful of Molasses 1/2 Cupful of Butter or Lard 1
Teaspoonful of Soda 1 Teaspoonful of Ginger

Boil the molasses five minutes. Remove from the fire, and
add soda, butter and ginger. When cooled a little, stir in the
flour until thick enough to roll, then roll thin as a postage-
stamp. Cut with a cooky-cutter, and bake in a hot oven,
being careful not to burn. Shut in a tin pail. These will keep
for a long time.

Gold Cake

1 Cupful of Sugar 1/2 Cupful of Butter Yolks of 4 Eggs
Whites of 1 Egg 1/2 Cupful of Milk 1/2 Teaspoonful of
Cream of Tartar 1/4 Teaspoonful of Soda 1-3/4 Cupfuls of
Flour Flavoring

Cream butter and sugar together. Add the well-beaten eggs,
milk, flavoring and flour into which the cream of tartar and
soda have been stirred. Bake thirty minutes in a moderate
oven.

Hermits

1 Cupful of Sugar 1/2 Cupful of Molasses 2/3 Cupful of
Butter 2 Eggs 1 Cupful of Raisins, Chopped Fine 2
Tablespoonfuls of Milk 1 Teaspoonful of Soda 1
Teaspoonful of Cinnamon 1 Teaspoonful of Nutmeg 1/2
Teaspoonful of Cloves Flour enough to roll

Cream the butter and sugar together, beat the eggs, add to the butter and sugar, then stir in the molasses, milk and spices. Add the raisins which have been covered with flour, and, last of all, the flour into which the dry soda has been sifted. Roll thin and cut with cooky-cutter.

Jumbles

2 Cupfuls of Sugar 1 Cupful of Butter 1/2 Cupful of Milk 2 Eggs 1 Teaspoonful of Soda 2 Teaspoonfuls of Cream of Tartar 1 Teaspoonful of Lemon Flour enough to roll

Cream together the butter and sugar. Stir into the well-beaten egg. Add milk. Stir cream of tartar and soda into the flour, dry. Beat all together and flavor. Cut into rings and bake in a well-greased pan.

Nut Cake

1 Cupful of Sugar 1/2 Cupful of Butter 1/2 Cupful of Milk 2 Eggs 2 Cupfuls of Flour 1 Teaspoonful of Cream of Tartar 1/2 Teaspoonful of Soda 1 Cupful of Hickory Nut Meats, or English Walnuts

Cream the butter and sugar together, then add the well-beaten eggs and milk and put the soda and cream of tartar into the flour. Stir all together, adding nut meats, covered with flour, last.

Oatmeal Cookies

2 Eggs 1 Cupful of Sugar 1 1/2 Cupfuls of Oatmeal or
Rolled Oats 2/3 Cupful of Cocoanut 1/4 Teaspoonful of
Salt 1/2 Teaspoonful of Vanilla 2 Tablespoonfuls of Butter

Cream the butter and sugar together and add the well-
beaten eggs. Add the remainder of the ingredients and drop
on a well-greased baking-pan. Bake in a moderate oven,
from fifteen to twenty minutes.

One, Two, Three, Four Cake

1 Cupful of Butter 2 Cupfuls of Sugar 3 Cupfuls of Flour 4
Eggs 2/3 Cupful of Milk 2 Teaspoonfuls of Cream of Tartar
1 Teaspoonful of Soda

Cream the butter and sugar together and add the well-
beaten eggs; beat all and add milk; beat again. Sift the
cream of tartar and the soda into the flour; stir all together.
Bake in a slow oven. This will make two loaves.

Ribbon Cake

3 Eggs 2 Cupfuls of Sugar 2/3 Cupful of Butter 1 Cupful of
Milk 3 Cupfuls of Flour 1 Teaspoonful of Cream of Tartar
1 Tablespoonful of Molasses A little Salt and flavor,
Lemon or Almond 1 Large Cupful of Raisins 1/4 Pound of
Citron 1 Teaspoonful of Cinnamon and Cloves A little
Nutmeg 1/2 Teaspoonful of Soda

Cream the butter and sugar together, and add the well-beaten eggs and the milk. Mix the salt, soda and cream of tartar, with the flour. Stir all together. Put half of this mixture into two oblong pans. To the remainder add one tablespoonful of molasses, one large cupful of raisins, stoned and chopped, a quarter of a pound of citron sliced thin, one teaspoonful of cinnamon and cloves, a little nutmeg, and one tablespoonful of flour. Bake in two pans of the same size as used for the first half. Put the sheets together while warm, alternately, with jelly between.

Roll Jelly Cake

4 Eggs 1 Cupful of Sugar 1 Cupful of Flour 1 Teaspoonful of Cream of Tartar 1/2 Teaspoonful of Soda Pinch of Salt 1 Teaspoonful of Extract of Lemon

Beat together eggs and sugar, add salt and extract. Stir into the dry flour the soda and cream of tartar. Mix all together. Bake in a moderate oven, in a large pan, and turn out, when done, on a clean towel, which has been sprinkled with powdered sugar. Spread with jelly and roll while warm.

Silver Cake

1 Cupful of Sugar 1/3 Cupful of Butter 2 Cupfuls of Flour Whites of 3 Eggs 1/2 Cupful of Milk 1 Scant Teaspoonful of Cream of Tartar 1/2 Teaspoonful of Soda Almond Flavoring

Cream together the butter and sugar, add milk and flavoring. Stir cream of tartar and soda into dry flour. Last of all add whites of eggs, beaten to a stiff froth. To make a very good cake, the butter and sugar should be creamed with the hand. Citron also makes it very nice.

Sponge Cake, No.1

3 Eggs 1 1/2 Cupfuls of Sugar 1/2 Cupful of Water Pinch of Salt 1 1/2 Cupfuls of Flour 1 Teaspoonful of Cream of Tartar 1/2 Teaspoonful of Soda

Beat eggs and sugar together, add water and salt, then put soda and cream of tartar into the dry flour. Beat all together. Bake slowly.

Sponge Cake, No. 2, Grandmother's Rule

4 Eggs Pinch of Salt 1 Cupful of Sugar 1 Cupful of Flour 1 Teaspoonful of Baking-powder

Beat the eggs ten minutes, add sugar, and beat again. Then add the flour, into which has been stirred the baking-powder. Stir all together and flavor. Bake in a moderate oven.

SOME OLD-FASHIONED CANDIES

Chocolate Taffy

1 1/2 Cupfuls of Molasses 1 1/2 Cupfuls of Sugar 1/2
Cupful of Milk 2 Squares of Chocolate 1 Small
Teaspoonful of Flour Butter the size of a Walnut

Stir the sugar, flour and grated chocolate into the molasses
and milk.

When hot add the butter. Boil until it strings. Pour into
buttered tin.

When nearly cold mark into squares.

Molasses Candy

2 Cupfuls of Molasses 2 Teaspoonfuls of Vinegar Butter
the size of a Walnut 1/4 Teaspoonful of Soda

Put the molasses, vinegar and butter into a saucepan. Boil
until it strings when dropped from a spoon, or until it is
brittle when dropped into cold water. Stir the soda in
briskly and pour into a buttered tin. When nearly cold, pull
until nearly white. Cut into small pieces or sticks and lay
on buttered platter.

Butter Scotch

1/2 Cupful of Molasses 1/2 Cupful of Sugar 1/2 Cupful of Butter

Boil until it strings. Pour into buttered tin and when cold break into pieces. This is very nice when cooled on snow.

Pop Corn Balls (very old recipe)

1 Cupful of Molasses Piece of Butter, half the size of an Egg

Boil together until it strings and then stir in a pinch of soda. Put this over a quart dish full of popped corn. When cool enough to handle squeeze into balls the size of an orange.

DESSERTS

Apple Tarts

Roll rich pie crust thin as for pies. Cut into rounds, pinch up the edge half an inch high and place in muffin rings. Put into each one a tablespoonful of apple sauce and bake in a hot oven for twenty minutes. Beat the white of an egg to a stiff froth and add two tablespoonfuls of sugar. Drop a spoonful on the top of each and brown quickly in a hot oven.

Baked Apples, No. 1

Take good, sour apples; greenings are best. Scoop out the cores, wash and place in a baking-pan. Fill the hole with sugar, and a tablespoonful for each apple besides. Pour over these a generous supply of cold water. Bake in a hot oven, until light and fluffy. These make a delicious dessert, if served with cream.

Baked Apples, No. 2

Wash, core and quarter sour apples. Put them into an earthen crock. Cover with cold water adding a cup and a half of sugar to six apples, or sweeten to taste. Bake three or four hours, until they are a dark amber color.

Baked Sweet Apples

Wash clean, fair, sweet apples. Put these into a baking-pan, with a little cold water and a half-cup of molasses, if four to six apples are used. Bake slowly until you can stick a fork through them. Years ago, people ate these, with crackers and milk. Baked apples and milk was a favorite dish.

Baked Apple Dumplings

Take rich pie crust, roll thin as for pie and cut into rounds as large as a tea plate. Pare and slice fine, one small apple for each dumpling. Lay the apple on the crust, sprinkle on a tiny bit of sugar and nutmeg, turn edges of crust over the apple and press together. Bake in a hot oven for twenty minutes. Serve hot with cold sauce.

Fried Apples

Pare and slice apples and fry in hot fat. When removed from the fire, sprinkle over them a little sugar. Bananas are nice cooked in the same way.

Bramberries

Crust 1 1/2 Cupfuls of Flour 1/2 Cupful of Lard (scant) 1 Teaspoonful of Salt Just enough Water to wet smooth

Filling 1 Cupful of Raisins 1 Cracker 1 Lemon 2/3 Cupful of Sugar 1 Egg A Little Salt

Beat the egg, add sugar, salt, lemon juice and grated rind. Roll cracker fine, chop raisins and mix all together. Roll the crust thin, cut into rounds. Put a spoonful of filling between two rounds and pinch the edges together. Prick top crust with fork. Bake in iron pan for twenty minutes.

Cream Puffs

1 Cupful of Hot Water 1/2 Cupful of Butter 1 Cupful of Flour 1 Pinch of Salt and Baking Soda 3 Eggs

Put the water and butter, into a dish on the stove.

When boiling, stir in the dry flour, into which you have put the salt and soda. Stir until smooth and thick. When nearly cool, add three eggs, one at a time. Drop on a buttered pan and bake twenty minutes in a hot oven. This will make twelve cakes. When they are cold, make a slit in the side with a sharp knife, and fill with whipped cream or the following mixture:

One pint of milk, one egg, two-thirds of a cupful of sugar, one large spoonful of flour. Beat the egg, sugar, flour, and a little salt together till smooth and stir into the boiling milk. Flavor with lemon.

Floating Island

1 Quart of Milk 4 Eggs 1 Cupful of Sugar 1 Teaspoonful of Cornstarch 1 Teaspoonful of Vanilla Pinch of Salt

Put the milk on the stove and heat to nearly the boiling point. Whip whites of the eggs to a stiff froth and drop them by spoonfuls into the hot milk for a few minutes to cook. With a skimmer remove these islands to a platte. Beat the yolks of the egg with sugar, salt and cornstarch. Stir into the milk until it boils. Flavor and cool. Turn into a glass dish and lay the "islands" on top of the custard. Serve cold.

Huckleberry Dumplings

2 Cupfuls of Flour 2 Teaspoonfuls of Cream of Tartar 1 Teaspoonful of Soda 1/2 Teaspoonful of Salt 1 Teaspoonful of Lard

Mix ingredients together with water until thick enough to roll. Cut into rounds an inch thick as for biscuits. Boil one quart of huckleberries in one-half pint of water and one-half cupful of sugar. Drop in the dumplings. Boil for twenty minutes. Serve with cold sauce or cream and sugar.

Coffee Jelly

1 Small Box of Gelatine 1 Pint of Strong Coffee 1 Cupful of Sugar 1 Scant Quart of Boiling Water Flavor with Vanilla

Soak the gelatine in cold water for fifteen minutes. Stir into the coffee and add sugar, salt and water, then vanilla. Pour into a mould and set away to cool. Serve with sweetened whipped cream.

Lemon Jelly

1/2 Box of Gelatine 1/2 Cupful of Cold Water 1-1/2 Cupfuls of Boiling Water 1 Cupful of Sugar 3 Lemons

Soak gelatine in the cold water for half an hour. Add boiling water, sugar and juice of lemons. Stir well and strain into mould or small cups.

Strawberry Shortcake, No. 1

1 Pint of Flour 1/3 Cupful of Lard A little Salt Milk enough to make a stiff dough 1 Box of Strawberries 2 Teaspoonfuls of Cream of Tartar 1 Teaspoonful of Soda

Put the salt, soda, lard and cream of tartar, into the dry flour, mix with milk (water will do), divide into halves and roll large enough for a Washington pie tin. Spread butter over one, lay the other on top, bake twenty minutes. Hull and wash and mash the berries and sweeten to taste. Separate the two cakes, butter, and place the berries between. Serve hot.

Strawberry Shortcake, No. 2

1 Tablespoonful of Butter 2/3 Cupful of Sugar 1 Egg 1/2
Cupful of Milk 1 Teaspoonful of Cream of Tartar 1/2
Teaspoonful of Soda 1 Box of Strawberries 1 Cupful of
Cream

Cream together the butter and sugar and add the well-
beaten egg and milk. Stir the cream of tartar and soda into
the dry flour and beat all together. Bake in two Washington
pie tins. Hull, wash, mash and sweeten to taste, the berries.
Put half of these between the two loaves, the other half on
top, with whipped cream on top of all.

EGGS

To Boil Eggs

Put your eggs into a bowl which can be sent to the table.
Pour boiling water over them and let stand eight or ten
minutes. It is essential that the water be boiling. This way
of boiling eggs, though so simple, is going out of fashion,
unfortunately, as it makes a wonderful difference in the
appearance of the egg when broken open, and above all, in
its digestibility. Eggs should never be boiled in any other
way for invalids.

Eggs on Toast

Toast as many slices of bread as desired. Butter well and
pour over these just enough salted water to soften. Have
ready a dish of boiling water. Stir it round and round with a
spoon or fork, break the egg and drop into this swirling
water. Remove from the water in from four to six minutes,
as preferred, and place one on each slice of bread. Serve
hot, with a dash of pepper, if liked.

Plain Omelette

2 Eggs 2 Teaspoonfuls of Water Pinch of Salt

Beat whites and yolks separately. Put together, salt, and
add water. Pour onto a hot buttered frying pan and fry one

side until it is puffed up, then turn half over and serve at once.

Ham Omelette

Make a plain omelette and add two-thirds of a cupful of chopped boiled ham. Pour into the hot frying pan and cook both sides.

New England Poached Eggs

4 Eggs 8 Tablespoonfuls of Milk Butter the size of a Walnut 1/2 Teaspoonful of Salt

Break the eggs into a sauce pan with milk, salt and butter. Cook until they thicken, stirring constantly. Remove from fire before it wheys. Serve hot with a dash of pepper.

FISH

Clam Fritters

1 Egg 1 Cupful of Milk 1 Cupful of Bread-flour and a Little Salt

Beat the egg and half the milk, adding the flour gradually, to make the batter smooth. Salt, and add the last half-cupful of milk. Put one clam into one teaspoonful of batter and drop into boiling lard. Serve hot.

Fish Balls

1 Cupful of Hot Mashed Potatoes 1/2 Cupful of Shredded Cod-fish 2 Teaspoonfuls of Melted Butter 2 Tablespoonfuls of Milk

Put the fish into a piece of cheese-cloth, let cold water run over it, and squeeze dry. Mix ingredients all together. Take a little flour in the hand and roll half a tablespoonful of the mixture between the palms, to the size of a small peach. Fry in deep fat.

To Boil a Lobster

Have a large kettle on the fire with plenty of boiling water, deep enough to cover the lobster well. Put into this one cupful of salt, if you cannot get the sea-water. When the water is galloping, put in the lobster, head foremost, and keep it under water. Boil from twenty to thirty-five minutes according to size.

To Dress Lobsters Cold

Crack the shell of the claws carefully, remove the meat and place on a platter. Turn the lobster on its back, lay a heavy knife on the middle of the tail, all the way up to the body. Give it a gentle blow with a hammer, then with both hands turn back the shell and draw out the tail intact. Twist off the claws from the under side of the body and remove the body from the shell. Open and remove the stomach and sandbags. Open the tail in length, halfway through, on the under side, remove the black vein from the body to the end. Dress with parsley and serve.

Baked Mackerel

1 Mackerel 3 Small Slices of Salt Pork Salt to Taste

Split open the mackerel, remove head and insides, wash clean, and lay in a baking-pan on a well buttered paper or cheese-cloth, the skin side down. Spread over this slices of salt pork and a little salt. Bake in moderate oven for twenty minutes, or half an hour. This is much nicer than fried mackerel.

Oysters on Toast

Toast as many slices of bread as you require. Wipe enough oysters to cover them and season with pepper and salt. Put a little hot water over the bread and place in a very hot oven, until the edges of the oysters curl. Serve hot, with a white sauce.

Baked Shad

Make a nice dressing of five or six crackers, according to size of family (bread crumbs will do). Roll fine, or soak until soft in milk (water will do). Season to taste with poultry dressing, salt and add a small piece of butter. Wash the shad and stuff. Have a large sheet of white paper, well buttered, or a piece of cheese-cloth. Put into a baking-pan and set in the oven. Bake one hour. Spanish mackerel is fine baked in the same way.

MEAT DISHES

A La Mode Beef

3 Pounds of Beef 6 Onions 4 or 5 White Turnips Potatoes Salt

Take three pounds of a cheap cut of beef. Wash, put into an iron pan, sprinkle over it salt to taste. Pare six onions, more or less, according to size of family, and prepare four or five small white turnips sliced thin. Lay these around the meat, and pour over all a quart of cold water. Put into the oven and bake three hours. Pare potatoes enough for the family, putting them in an hour and a half before serving. This is a most delicious way to cook beef. As the water cooks away, add more. Thicken the gravy, with flour wet with water, as you would with any roast meat.

Beefsteak Pie

2 Pounds of Beef (any cheap cut will do) 1 Onion 1 Tablespoonful of Salt

Cut the meat into small pieces; cover with cold water, salt and put into the oven; cut the onion into small pieces and add. Bake three hours in an earthen dish. Half an hour before serving, put over the top a crust, made of two cupfuls of flour, two heaping teaspoonfuls of baking-powder, one-half teaspoonful of salt, and one tablespoonful of lard. Wet with water or milk, as for biscuits.

Beef Stew with Dumplings

3 Pounds of Shin-bone with Meat 6 Potatoes 2 Large
Onions 1 Tablespoonful of Salt

Wash the meat, put into a kettle, cover with cold water and
boil four hours. Add the salt, and more water, as it boils
away. Pare the onions, wash and slice thin; put them in
with the boiling meat, allowing two hours for cooking. Pare
potatoes, wash, slice thin; put them in with the meat and
onions, allowing three-quarters of an hour for cooking.

Dumplings

2 Heaping Cupfuls of Flour 2 Teaspoonfuls of Cream of
Tartar 1 Teaspoonful of Baking Soda 1 Teaspoonful of
Lard 1 Teaspoonful of Salt 1 Glass of Water

Roll out an inch thick and cut into round pieces. Put these
on a wire plate, on top of the meat; cover and let boil
twenty minutes. Lift them out, and thicken the stew with
three dessertspoonfuls of flour, wet with a scant cup of
water.

New England Boiled Dinner

This consists of corned beef, white and sweet potatoes,
cabbage, beets, turnips, squash, parsnips and carrots. The
quantity depends upon the size of the family. Eight pounds
of meat is sufficient for a family of eight. Boil the meat
four hours, the beets three hours, the cabbage one and a

half hours, squash and turnips three-quarters of an hour. Boil these in one kettle, all together. Beets, carrots and parsnips should be boiled with the skin on. Pare the potatoes, pare and slice the squash and turnip. Pick the outer leaves from cabbage and cut in quarters. When done, pare parsnips and carrots. Drop the beets into cold water and slip the skin off with the hand.

Brunswick Stew

1 Chicken or 3 Pounds of Lamb 1 Onion 4 Potatoes 4 Ears of Corn Salt and Pepper 6 Tomatoes

Cook the chicken or lamb until tender in two quarts of water. Take from the water and chop fine. Put back in the liquor, add the corn, cut from the cob, tomatoes, onion, and potatoes all chopped, salt and pepper to taste. Cook two hours. In winter this can be made by using canned corn and tomatoes.

How to Corn Beef

A piece of fresh beef weighing seven or eight pounds is sufficient for a family of eight. Wash, clean and put it in an earthen dish, twenty-four hours before cooking. Cover with cold water, and add a cup and a half of ice-cream salt. When ready to cook it, remove from the brine and wash, placing it in cold water. Cook four hours.

Corn Beef Hash

Corned Beef

Milk

Potatoes

Salt and Pepper

Lump of Butter

Chop the meat fine, add the same bulk of potatoes or a little more. Put into a saucepan or spider a lump of butter the size of an egg, and a few spoonfuls of milk or water. When bubbling, put in the meat and potatoes, and a little salt and pepper, if you like. Stir for a while, then let it stand ten or fifteen minutes, until a crust is formed at the bottom. Loosen from the pan with a cake-turner. Turn a warm platter over it. Turn pan and hash together quickly and serve. If you have a scant quantity, place it on slices of toasted bread, which have been buttered and wet with hot water.

Breaded Pork Chops

6 Chops 1 Cupful of Bread Crumbs 1 Egg Pinch of Salt 1/2 Cupful of Milk

Beat the egg and milk together, adding the salt. Dip the chops into this mixture, then into the crumbs. Fry in hot fat. Veal cutlets can be served in the same way.

Potted Beef

3 Pounds of a Cheap Cut of Beef 1/2 Can of Tomatoes Salt to taste 3 Onions

Put the meat into a kettle, cover with cold water and boil slowly for three or four hours. Add salt and onions, cut fine. Put the tomato through a colander. Boil all together, and, as the water boils away, add more. Serve the meat hot. The liquor makes a delicious soup, thickened with two tablespoonfuls of flour.

A Fine Way to Cook Veal

2 Pounds of Veal, or according to size of family

1 Egg

Bread Crumbs

Milk, Salt and Pepper

Cut the veal into small pieces, a good size for serving, and season with salt and pepper. Dip into the egg, which has been beaten light, then into the bread crumbs. Have a little pork fat (lard will do) in a frying-pan, and cook until brown. Set on the back of the stove and cook slowly for ten minutes. Cover with milk, and bake in the oven very slowly for one hour in a covered pan. The toughest veal, cooked in this way, will be as tender as chicken.

Veal Patties

1 1/2 Cupfuls of Boiled Rice 1 Cupful of Veal 1 Teaspoonful of Salt 1/2 Teaspoonful of Poultry Dressing 1 Egg 1 Tablespoonful of Milk

Grind or chop the veal, salt and stir into the rice with the dressing; beat the eggs, add milk, and stir all together. Drop a tablespoonful spread out thin on the griddle, and fry as you would griddle-cakes. Chicken, pork, or lamb may be used instead of veal.

MISCELLANEOUS

Boston Baked Beans

Pick over and wash three cupfuls of small white beans; cover with cold water and soak over night. In the morning, put them on the stove, just to scald, not boil, in the same water. Pour off the water and put into an earthen bean-pot. Add seven teaspoonfuls of sugar, one teaspoonful of salt, one half-pound of salt pork, fat and lean mixed. Cover with water, and bake from eight A.M. until six P.M. As the water boils away add more.

A Breakfast Dish

Take stale brown bread, no matter how dry, and boil until it is soft like pudding. Serve hot, with cream.

Cracker Tea for Invalids

Take four Boston crackers, split open, toast to a delicate brown on each side. Put these into a bowl, or earthen dish of some kind, pour over them a quart of boiling water. Let it stand on the back of the stove half an hour. When cold, give two or three teaspoonfuls to the patient. It is nourishing, and the stomach will retain it when absolutely nothing else can be taken.

Crust Coffee

Take the crusts, or any pieces of stale brown bread, and bake in the oven until hard and brown. Put them into an agate or earthen tea-pot, pour over them boiling water and boil ten or fifteen minutes. Strain and serve hot like any coffee, with cream and sugar.

Grape Juice

10 Pounds of Grapes 3 Pounds of Sugar 1 Cupful of Water

Pick from the stems, and wash clean, ten pounds of grapes. Put them on the stove in a kettle, with a little water, and cook until tender. Strain through a flannel bag. Do not squeeze it. Return juice to the kettle, add sugar, and boil for five minutes. Seal in glass jars when boiling hot. Slant the jars, when filling, to prevent cracking. When serving, add nearly the same amount of water.

Mince Meat

4 Cupfuls of Chopped Meat 12 Cupfuls of Chopped Apples 2 Cupfuls of Chopped Suet 1 Cupful of Vinegar 3 Cupfuls Seeded Raisins 1 Cupful of Currants 5 Cupfuls of Brown Sugar 1 1/2 Cupfuls of Molasses 6 Teaspoonfuls of Cinnamon 3 Teaspoonfuls of Cloves 1 Teaspoonful of Nutmeg 1/4 Pound of Citron Rind and Juice of One Lemon Butter the size of an Egg and Salt

Moisten with cold coffee or strong tea. Cook slowly two hours.

Home-made Potato Yeast

4 Good-Sized Potatoes 1 Quart of Boiling Water 2/3 Cupful of Sugar 1/3 Cupful of Salt 1 1/2 Cupfuls of Old Yeast

Boil, peel and mash the potatoes; add the boiling water, sugar and salt. If old yeast cannot be obtained, use one and one-half cakes of compressed yeast. Put this into a pitcher or dish which will hold three pints; place in a warm spot to rise; keep covered. Use two-thirds of a cupful to one quart of flour. This recipe has been in use over fifty years.

PICKLES

Pickled Cauliflower

1 Cauliflower 2 Tablespoonfuls of Salt Cloves 1 Quart of
Vinegar 1 Teaspoonful of Whole Cloves 1 Teaspoonful of
White Mustard Seed

Pull the cauliflower into pieces, put into cold water with
the salt, heat gradually and boil five minutes, then drain
until dry. Put this into a glass jar. Boil the clove and
mustard seed in the vinegar, and pour over the cauliflower,
hot. Have it covered with vinegar. Seal while hot.

Green Chopped Pickle, No. 1

1 Peck of Green Tomatoes 6 Large Onions 4 Green Peppers
2 Red Peppers 2 Pounds of Brown Sugar 4 Bunches of
Celery 3 Pints of Vinegar 2 Tablespoonfuls of Allspice 2
Tablespoonfuls of Whole Cloves 2 Sticks of Cinnamon

Put the tomatoes, onions and peppers through the meat-
grinder, or chop fine, and sprinkle over them one cupful of
salt. Let stand over night. In the morning drain off the
water, put in the other ingredients and let come to the
boiling point, then add one ten-cent bottle of horse-radish.
Seal in jars having a glass top.

Green Chopped Pickle, No. 2

1 Peck of Green Tomatoes 2 Large Cauliflowers 1 Head of
White Cabbage 3 Pounds of Sugar Vinegar 6 Red Peppers
(Seeded) 5 Large Onions 1 Cupful of Salt 1/2 Ounce of
White Mustard Seed 1/2 Ounce of Whole Cloves 1/2
Ounce of Celery Seed 1 Dessertspoonful of Ground Mace

Put through the meat-grinder, or chop, tomatoes,
cauliflower, cabbage, onions, and peppers. Sprinkle over
these one cupful of salt and let stand over night. In the
morning drain off water, cover with vinegar, and add the
other ingredients. Cook until tender.

Chili Sauce, No. 1

6 Ripe Tomatoes 1 Onion 4 Green Peppers 1 Tablespoonful
of Sugar 1 Tablespoonful of Salt 1 1/2 Cupfuls of Vinegar

Chop, or put through the meat-grinder, tomatoes, peppers
and onions, add sugar, salt and vinegar. Boil one hour and
seal in jars.

Chili Sauce, No. 2

1 Quart of Ripe Tomatoes 1 Cupful of Cider Vinegar 1
Onion 1 Red Pepper 2 Teaspoonfuls of Salt 2 Teaspoonfuls
of White Sugar

Chop, or put through the grinder, the onion and pepper, then add the other ingredients and cook one hour, uncovered.

Chili Sauce, No. 3

8 or 9 Large Ripe Tomatoes 1 Large Onion 2 Red Peppers 1 Teaspoonful of Cloves 1 Teaspoonful of Allspice 1 Nutmeg 1 Tablespoonful of Salt 2 Tablespoonfuls of Sugar 1 Teaspoonful of Ginger 1 Teaspoonful of Cinnamon 2 Small Cupfuls of Vinegar

Chop the onion and peppers fine, mix all together, and cook half an hour. Bottle while hot.

Chow Chow, No. 1

1/2 Peck Green Tomatoes 1 Large Head of Cabbage 6 Large Onions 1/2 Pint Grated Horseradish 1/4 Pound of White Mustard Seed 1/4 Cupful of Ground Black Pepper 1/2 Ounce of Celery Seed 2 Pounds of Brown Sugar 3 Quarts of Vinegar 1 Cupful of Salt

Chop or grind tomatoes, cabbage and onions, very fine and salt over night. Next day, drain off the brine, add vinegar and other ingredients, then mix well and put into glass jars. Do not cook.

Chow Chow, No. 2

1 Peck of Green Tomatoes 1 Cupful of Salt 6 Onions 6
Peppers 1 Cupful of Sugar Vinegar enough to cover 1
Tablespoonful of Cinnamon 1 Tablespoonful of Cloves 1
Tablespoonful of Allspice 1 Even Spoonful of Ginger

Cut the tomatoes, onions and peppers into small pieces. Put
the salt over them and let stand over night. Drain off the
liquor the next day and throw it away. Mix all together,
cover with vinegar and simmer until tender. Seal in glass
jars.

Cold Catsup

1 Peck of Ripe Tomatoes 2 Tablespoonfuls of Salt 1
Teacupful of White Mustard Seed 2 Teacupfuls of
Chopped or Ground Onions 1 Teacupful of Sugar 2
Tablespoonfuls of Pepper 4 Red Peppers 8 Celery Stalks,
or 2 Ounces of Celery Seed 2 Teaspoonfuls of Ground
Cloves 3 Pints of Vinegar

Drain the tomatoes well before mixing. Mix together, let
stand a few hours and it is ready for use.

Corn Relish

18 Ears of Corn 1 Onion 1 Cabbage 1/4 Pound of Mustard
1 Pint of Vinegar 4 Cupfuls of Sugar 1/2 Cupful of Salt 2
Peppers

Cut the corn from the cob, chop onion, peppers and cabbage, add sugar, salt and vinegar, and cook slowly three-quarters of an hour. Ten minutes before taking from the fire, add a very scant fourth of a pound of dissolved mustard. Seal in glass jars.

Home-Made Cucumber Pickles

Take enough small cucumbers to fill four one-quart jars; wash and sprinkle over them one cupful of table salt; let them remain over night; in the morning, wash and pack in the jars. Add one teaspoonful of whole cloves, one teaspoonful of whole allspice, one teaspoonful of white mustard seed, and two pieces of alum, as large as a pea, to each jar. Fill the jars with boiling vinegar, and seal.

Quickly Made Cucumber Pickle

Take small cucumbers, wipe clean and lay them in a small jar or stone crock. Allow one quart of coarse salt to a pail of water. Boil the salt and water until the salt is dissolved, skim and pour boiling hot on the cucumbers. Cover them tight, and let them stand twenty-four hours, then turn out and drain. Boil as much vinegar as will cover the cucumbers, skimming thoroughly. Put the cucumbers into clean glass jars and pour the vinegar on boiling hot. Put in a piece of alum the size of a bean, and seal. They will be ready for use in forty-eight hours. Add peppers and spice if desired.

Mixed Pickles

2 Quarts of Green Tomatoes 2 Quarts of Cucumbers 2
Quarts of Small Onions 2 Heads of Cauliflower 2 Green
Peppers 1 Gallon of Vinegar 1/2 Pound of Ground Mustard
3 Cupfuls of Sugar 1 Ounce of Tumeric Powder 1 Cupful
of Flour 1 Cupful of Salt

Cut the tomatoes, cucumbers, onions, cauliflower and
peppers into small pieces. Pour over them boiling brine,
made of three quarts of water and one cupful of salt. Let
this stand twenty-four hours, then pour off the brine. Stir
the flour, mustard, sugar and tumeric powder together, and
wet with a little of the vinegar, then stir it into the boiling
vinegar, as you would make gravy. Put the other
ingredients in, and simmer together until all are tender.
Seal in glass jars.

Piccalilli, No. 1

1 Peck of Green Tomatoes 1 1/2 Cupfuls of Sugar 1/2
Cupful of Salt 3 Pints of Vinegar 2 Large Spoonfuls of
Ground Cloves 1/2 Pint of Green Peppers

Chop all together and simmer three hours.

Piccalilli, No. 2

1 Peck of Green Tomatoes 1 Ounce of Whole Cloves,
Allspice, and Mustard Seed 4 Onions 2 Green Peppers
Vinegar to cover 1 Cupful of Salt

Slice the tomatoes, sprinkle over the salt, and let stand over night. In the morning, pour off the water and drain. Slice peppers and onions, tie the spices in a piece of cheese-cloth, put all together, and pour over the vinegar. Let simmer three or four hours, and seal in glass jars. Very good, and not sweetened.

Piccalilli, No. 3

1 Peck of Green Tomatoes 4 Green Peppers Allspice, Cloves and Mustard Seed 1 Cupful of Salt 6 Onions Vinegar

Wipe clean, cut into small pieces, sprinkle over them a cupful of salt, and let stand over night. In the morning, drain off the liquor, add six onions, four green peppers, sliced thin, one ounce each, of whole allspice, cloves, and white mustard seed. Tie the spices in a muslin bag, cover with vinegar, and cook three or four hours slowly, until very tender, in an agate kettle. This is much nicer if sealed in glass jars.

Tomato Catsup, No. 1

1 Peck of Ripe Tomatoes 6 Cupfuls of Vinegar 8 Onions 2 Cupfuls of Sugar 6 Red Peppers 1/2 Cupful of Salt

Chop or grind onions and peppers. Put with tomatoes, stew and press through colander, then add the rest of the ingredients and boil until it is thick. Seal while hot in glass jars.

Tomato Catsup, No. 2

1 Pint of Vinegar 2 Quarts of Ripe Tomatoes 1
Tablespoonful of Salt 1 Tablespoonful of Mustard 1
Tablespoonful of Black Pepper Allspice 2 Pods Red Pepper

Peel the tomatoes, add salt, black pepper, mustard, red
pepper, and allspice. Mix and stew slowly, in the vinegar
for two hours. Strain through a sieve, and cook until you
have one quart. Cork in bottles.

Pickled Watermelon Rind

Pare off the green rind and all the pink, using just the white
of the melon. Cut into large squares. Cover with water, and
put in a pinch of alum. Let stand twenty-four hours. Pour
off the water and drain. Take enough vinegar to cover, add
one teaspoonful of whole allspice, cloves and white
mustard seed, and pour over the rind boiling hot. Heat the
vinegar three mornings in succession, and pour over the
rind while hot. It will be ready for use in a week.

PIES

Rich Pie Crust

3 Cupfuls of Flour 1 Cupful of Lard 1 Dessertspoonful of
Salt

Put salt and lard into the flour, working in the lard with the
hand until thoroughly mixed. Add enough water to barely
wet,—ice-cold water is best. This is sufficient for two pies.

Pork Apple Pie

4 Apples 4 Tablespoonfuls of Sugar 1 Teaspoonful of
Ground Cinnamon 12 Pieces of Fat Salt Pork, size of a Pea

Line a pie-plate with rich crust; pare, core and slice apples
thin, to fill the plate; sprinkle over these the sugar,
cinnamon and pork; cover with crust and bake in moderate
oven. To be eaten warm.

Chocolate Custard Pie

1 Pint of Milk 4 Tablespoonfuls of Sugar 3 Eggs Pinch of
Salt 2 Tablespoonfuls of Cocoa or 1 Square of Chocolate 1
Teaspoonful of Vanilla

Beat yolks of eggs and add sugar and salt. Wet the cocoa
with half a cup of warm milk and stir into the yolks. Flavor.
Line a deep pie-plate with rich pie-crust, pinching a little

edge around the plate. Pour in the mixture and bake until it rises. Beat the whites to a stiff froth, add two tablespoonfuls of sugar, spread over the pie and brown in a hot oven.

Cocoanut Pie

1 Pint of Milk 3 Eggs Pinch of Salt 1/2 Cupful of Grated Cocoanut Piece of Butter the size of a Marble

Beat the yolks of the eggs, add sugar and salt and beat again. Put in the butter which has been melted, milk and cocoanut. Line a deep pie-plate with pie-crust and pour in the mixture. Bake until it rises—this is not nice if baked too long. Beat the whites of the eggs stiff and put on top of pie when it is cool. Set in the oven to brown.

Cranberry Pie

1 Quart of Cranberries 2 1/2 Cupfuls of Water 2 Cupfuls of Sugar

Line a deep pie-plate with crust. Put the cranberries on the stove, with the water, and cook until tender, then rub them through a colander. Put in two scant cupfuls of sugar, and boil for fifteen minutes. When cool, pour this into the plate, lay narrow strips of pie-crust from the center to the outer edge, and bake in a hot oven.

Cream Pie

1 Cupful of Sweet Cream White of One Egg 2/3 Cupful of Sugar 1 Teaspoonful of Vanilla

Bake with two crusts. Beat white of egg till stiff; add sugar, beat again; stir in the cream and flavor.

Old-Time Custard Pie

1 Pint of Milk 3 Eggs 4 Tablespoonfuls of Sugar 1/2 Teaspoonful of Salt

Line a deep plate with pie-crust, rolling it large enough to pinch up a little edge around the plate. Beat the eggs thoroughly, add sugar and salt, and beat again; then add the milk and stir well. Pour into the plate. Bake until it rises, being sure to remove from the oven before it wheys. Grate over the top a little nutmeg. The quality of the pie depends largely on the baking.

Frosted Lemon Pie

1 Lemon 1 Cupful of Sugar 1 1/2 Cupfuls of Milk 3 Eggs 2 Tablespoonfuls of Flour

Beat the yolks of the eggs, add the flour, the juice and rind of the lemon. Beat all together, add a little of the milk, and sugar; beat, then add the rest of the milk. Line a plate with crust, the same as for custard; pour in this mixture and bake, being careful not to let it whey when it is done. Beat the whites of the eggs to a stiff froth, add two tablespoonfuls of sugar, spread over the top, and set in the oven to brown.

Mock Mince Pie

1 1/2 Crackers 1 Cupful of Raisins 1/2 Cupful of Molasses 1/2 Cupful of Sugar 1/3 Cupful of Vinegar 1 Cupful of Steeped Tea 1 Egg Spices of all kinds (1/2 Teaspoonful of each)

Pumpkin Pie, No. 1

3 Cupfuls of Pumpkin (the bright yellow kind preferred) 3 Eggs 1 1/2 Cupfuls of Sugar 1 Heaping Tablespoonful of Flour 1 Teaspoonful of Cinnamon 1/2 Teaspoonful of Nutmeg 1 Quart of Milk, a little Salt

Boil the pumpkin till very tender and press through a colander. Mix all ingredients together. Line two deep pie-plates with a nice crust, and pour in the mixture, and bake until they rise.

Pumpkin Pie, No. 2

2 Cupfuls of Stewed and Sifted Pumpkin 2 Crackers Rolled Fine Boston Crackers or 3 Uneedas 1 Cupful of Sugar Pinch of Salt 1/2 Teaspoonful of Cinnamon 1 Pint of Milk

Pour the mixture into a deep pie-plate lined with crust, and bake in a slow oven one hour.

Rhubarb Pie

1 Pint of Rhubarb 1 Tablespoonful of Flour 1 Cupful of Sugar 1/4 Teaspoonful of Soda

Remove the skin, and cut into small pieces enough rhubarb to fill a pint bowl. Add the soda, and pour over it boiling water to cover. Let stand fifteen minutes and pour off the water. Line a deep plate with a rich crust. Put in the rhubarb, sugar and flour, cover with crust. Bake twenty minutes or half an hour.

Rolley Polys

Roll pie crust very thin and cut into strips four inches long and three inches wide. Over these spread jelly and lap the crust over, pressing edges together. Brush over the top with milk and sprinkle over a little sugar. Bake fifteen minutes.

Squash Pie

2 Cupfuls of Squash 5 Tablespoonfuls of Sugar 1 Tablespoonful of Flour 2 Cupfuls of Milk 1 Teaspoonful of Ground Cinnamon 1/4 Teaspoonful of Salt 1 Egg

Pare the squash, boil till tender, and sift through a colander. Beat the egg, add sugar, flour, cinnamon and salt. Stir these into the squash and add the milk, stirring in slowly. Bake in a deep plate, like a custard pie.

Cream Washington Pies

1 Egg 1/2 Cupful of Sugar 1 Cupful of Flour 1/2 Cupful of Milk (scant) 2 Tablespoonfuls of Melted Butter 1 Rounding Teaspoonful of Cream of Tartar 1/2 Teaspoonful of Soda

Cream butter and sugar together, add the well-beaten egg; then the milk into which has been stirred the soda and cream of tartar; last of all, the flour. Bake in three round shallow dishes.

Cream for Filling

1 Cupful of Milk 1 Egg A Little Salt 1 Heaping Tablespoonful of Flour 2 Tablespoonfuls of Sugar 1/2 Teaspoonful of Vanilla

Put the milk on the stove to heat. Put the sugar, flour and salt into the well-beaten egg and stir into the milk when boiling. When cool, add vanilla and spread between the layers of cake.

PRESERVES

Crab Apple Jelly

Cover the apples with water and boil until tender. Strain through a flannel bag. Boil the juice twenty minutes. Add the same amount of sugar, pint for pint, and cook five minutes. Pour into tumblers, and when cold, cover with paraffine.

California Jam

Divide and seed as many oranges as desired.

Slice thin, the pulp and skin together. Add to each pound of oranges one lemon, sliced thin, and one quart of cold water. Let all stand twenty-four hours; then cook until tender, with the same amount of sugar.

Canned Cherries

1 Quart of Cherries 1 Cupful of Sugar 1 Cupful of Water

Pick over and wash the cherries. If they are to be used for sauce, can them whole; if to be used for pies and puddings, remove stones and use less water, as there will be juice enough to cook them in. Cook until tender and seal when boiling hot.

Cherry Conserve

4 Pounds of Cherries 4 Pounds of Sugar 3 Oranges 1
Lemon

Wash and stone the cherries. Wash and remove seeds from
oranges and lemon. Put them through the meat-grinder or
chop fine. Cook all together twenty minutes, or until thick.
Put into tumblers and cover with paraffine.

Preserved Citron

4 Pounds of Citron 3 Pounds of Sugar 3 Gills of Water 3
Lemons

Pare the citron and cut into pieces one inch square. Cover
with cold water, adding a pinch of salt. Next day throw off
this water and cover with fresh water, this time adding a
pinch of alum. Slice the lemons, removing every seed, and
boil until tender. Boil the sugar and water together, skim,
then put into the syrup citron and lemon. Boil until it looks
rich and transparent. Skim out the fruit into jars or
tumblers, boil down the syrup for ten or fifteen minutes,
and pour over the fruit. If jars are used, fill to the brim and
seal while hot. This can be made in the summer from
watermelon-rind. Cut off all the pink of the melon, pare,
and prepare as you would citron. It is really very nice.

Currant Jelly

Pick currants from the stems and wash clean. Put them into a kettle with a very little water and cook for ten minutes. Strain through a flannel bag. Use one pint of juice to one pint of sugar. Boil the juice fifteen minutes, add sugar and boil five minutes. Pour into tumblers or jelly moulds, and when cold cover with paraffine.

Spiced Currants

5 Pounds of Currants 4 Pounds of Sugar 1 Pint of Vinegar 4 Teaspoonfuls of Cinnamon 4 Teaspoonfuls of Cloves

Boil slowly two and a half hours. Tie the spices in a cloth before boiling.

Cranberry Jelly

1 Quart of Cranberries 3 1/2 Cupfuls of Sugar

Put one quart of cranberries on the stove, with cold water enough to cover. Boil until tender. Strain through a colander. To this four cupfuls of juice add three and a half cupfuls of sugar. Boil, twenty minutes and turn into a mould which has been wet with cold water.

Grape Conserve

5 Pints of Grapes 8 Cupfuls of Sugar 1/2 Pound of Raisins
2 Oranges 1 Cupful of Nut Meats

Pick the grapes from the stems, wash, and separate the
pulps from the skins. Stew the pulps and press through a
colander. Put the raisins and oranges through the meat
grinder, after removing seeds. Cook all together except the
nuts. Add these about ten minutes before removing from
fire. Put into glasses and cover with paraffine. This makes
eleven glasses.

Grape Marmalade

When making grape-juice, use the grape which is left after
straining, for marmalade. Press through a colander,
measure and use the same amount of sugar. Cook until it
thickens and put into tumblers. When cold, cover with
paraffine.

Grape Preserve

Pick from the stems and wash the amount of grapes
desired. Squeeze the pulps from the skins. Put into a kettle
with very little water and boil until the seeds loosen. Press
through a colander. Put this with skins, weigh, and use
three-fourths of a pound of sugar, for every pound of fruit.
Cook all together until the skins are tender, usually about
an hour. Seal in glass jars.

Orange Marmalade

1 Grapefruit 1 Whole Orange Juice of Two Oranges 1
Whole Lemon Juice of Two Lemons

Chop fruit fine or put through the grinder. Measure and put
three times the amount of water. Let this stand till the next
day. Boil ten minutes. Stand again till the next day.
Measure and add equal amount of sugar. Boil until it jells.
This will make eleven or twelve tumblerfuls. Pour into
glasses while warm. When cold, pour over a thin coating of
paraffine.

Peach Marmalade

When preserving peaches or quinces, wipe them very clean
before paring, and save the skins for marmalade. Cook in
water enough to cover well and, when tender, press through
a colander. Measure, and add the same amount of sugar.
Boil half an hour, or until it thickens. Put into tumblers and
cover with paraffine. This is nice for school sandwiches, or
for filling for Washington pie or queen's pudding.

To Can Peaches

1 Quart of Peaches 1 Cupful of Sugar 2 Cupfuls of Water

Be sure to have the jars perfectly clean and warm. Glass
covers are always preferable. Make a syrup of the sugar
and water. Boil this hard for five minutes. Set back on the
stove and let it settle, then skim very thoroughly. Pare, cut

in half, and remove the stones from the peaches. When the syrup comes to a boil, put in enough peaches to fill your jar, whatever the size. Boil until tender enough to pierce with a wisp. Take the fruit out carefully with a spoon and place in the jar. Fill the jar with the boiling syrup, being careful always to cant the jar as you pour it in. If you do this, the jar will never crack, as it is likely to do if held perfectly straight or upright. Always run around the inside of the jar with a silver knife, and you will have no trouble in keeping fruit. Seal while hot. The peaches may be canned whole, if preferred.

Pickled Peaches

4 Pounds of Sugar 1 Pint of Vinegar 1 Tablespoonful of Cloves 1 Tablespoonful of Allspice Stick of Cinnamon

Boil the ingredients together for ten minutes before putting in the peaches. Cook as many peaches in this as possible, and have juice enough to fill up the jars. Tie the spices in a piece of cheese-cloth. Pears may be cooked in the same way.

Ginger Pears

10 Pounds of Pears 7 Pounds of Sugar 4 Lemons 6 Oranges 1 Box of Crystallized Ginger

Wipe pears clean and cut fine with sugar. Simmer an hour. Then add the lemons and oranges, seeded and cut fine, and the crystallized ginger. Let all boil together two or three hours.

Preserved Pears

1 Quart of Pears 1 Cupful of Sugar 2 Cupfuls of Water

Use pears which are just right to eat. Pare and drop into cold water, to prevent discoloring. Make a syrup of one cupful of sugar and two cupfuls of cold water, and boil the pears in this until you can stick a straw through them. Fill the jars with the fruit, all you can put in, then hold the jar slanting and fill with syrup to the very brim. Use whole pears, if preferred. If cut in halves, remove the core.

Way to Pickle Pears

1 Pint of Vinegar 3 Pounds of Sugar 6 Pounds of Pears 1/2 Tablespoonful of Cinnamon 1/2 Tablespoonful of whole Allspice 1 Tablespoonful of whole Cloves

Boil pears until tender. Boil vinegar, sugar, and spices together fifteen minutes, then put in the boiled pears, and cook all together half an hour. These will be nicer if sealed in glass jars.

To Preserve Pineapple

Peel the pineapple, remove the eyes and cut into small cubes. Weigh, and take three-fourths of a pound of sugar to one pound of fruit. Allow one cupful of water for each jar, and cook all together slowly until tender. Fill the jars. This is very nice for ice-cream or sherbet.

Quince Jelly

Pare, core, and quarter the fruit, and boil in water enough to cover. When soft, take out the fruit and strain the syrup through a flannel bag, then return the syrup to the kettle and boil until perfectly clear, skimming constantly. Measure syrup, adding an equal quantity of sugar, and boil twenty minutes, removing the scum which rises to the surface. Pour into tumblers or moulds and set aside to cool; then pour over the top a covering of paraffine.

Quince Marmalade

Put the quinces, which were boiled in water for the jelly, in with the cores and skins. Cover with water and boil ten or fifteen minutes. Press all through a colander. Measure, and add the same amount of sugar. Set on the stove and boil fifteen minutes, being careful not to scorch. Put into tumblers and cover with paraffine.

Quince Sauce

Peel, core, and cut into quarters the quinces. Boil in clear water until tender. Weigh the quinces before cooking, and put into the water in which they have been boiled three-fourths of a pound of sugar for every pound of quince. Boil five minutes and skim. Then put in the quinces and cook until of a dark amber color-for about an hour. As quinces are expensive, old-fashioned people used to put in one-fourth as much sweet apple or pear.

Raspberry Jam, No. I

Mash the berries, add equal parts of sugar, and let stand half an hour. Put on the stove in a kettle containing a half cupful of water, to prevent sticking. Boil until it thickens. Put into tumblers and cover with paraffine. Blackberries and strawberries used in the same way are very nice.

Raspberry Jam, No. 2

Mash the berries, and use two-thirds as much currant juice as you have berries. Measure, and add the same amount of sugar. Cook all together until it jells. Put into tumblers and cover with paraffine.

To Keep Rhubarb Through the Winter

Fill preserve jars with cold water. Cut the rhubarb into small pieces, as you would for a pie, and drop them into the jars. As they fill, the water will overflow. When full, screw the tops on the jars and set away. The water excludes the air, and the fruit, treated in this way, will keep for months. When required for use drain off the water and cook in the usual way.

Rhubarb Marmalade

5 Pounds of Rhubarb 5 Pounds of Sugar 5 Lemons, Juice and Rind 1 Pound of Chopped Walnuts 2 Teaspoonfuls of Extract of Jamaica Ginger

Cook all the ingredients, excepting the nuts and ginger, together three or four hours. Ten minutes before removing from the fire, add the ginger and nuts. Seal in glass jars, or put into tumblers. If tumblers are used, cover over the tops with a coating of paraffine.

Rhubarb Jam

6 Stalks of Rhubarb 3 Oranges 1 Lemon 4 Cupfuls of Sugar

Cook the rhubarb and rind and juice of the lemon and oranges together for twenty-five minutes. Put into tumblers and cover with paraffine.

Spiced Fruit

6 Pounds of Fruit 4 Pounds of Sugar 1 Pint of Vinegar

For all kinds of spiced fruit use the above measurements, adding one tablespoonful each of cinnamon, allspice, and cloves, and cook until tender. Seal in glass jars.

Bread Pudding

1 Pint of Stale Bread 1 Quart of Milk 1 Cupful of Sugar 1 Egg 1/2 Cupful of Raisins 1 Teaspoonful of Cinnamon 1/2 Teaspoonful of Salt

Pour hot water over the stale bread and let soak until soft. Then add other ingredients and bake for three hours in a moderate oven. If eaten cold, serve with hot sauce. If eaten hot, serve with cold sauce.

Steamed Chocolate Pudding

Butter size of a Walnut 1/2 Cupful of Sugar 1/2 Cupful of Milk 1 Cupful of Flour 1 Teaspoonful of Baking-powder 1 Square of Chocolate, or Two Dessertspoonfuls of Cocoa 1 Egg Salt to Taste

Cream together the butter and sugar, then add egg and milk; then the cocoa, flour, salt, and flavoring. Steam for an hour and a half, and serve hot with sauce.

Graham Pudding

1 1/2 Cupfuls of Graham Flour 1/2 Cupful of Molasses 1/2 Cupful of Milk 1/4 Cupful of Butter 1 Egg 1 Teaspoon of Soda 1/2 Cupful of Raisins and Currants, mixed Salt and Spice to taste

Stir the soda into the molasses, then add the beaten egg and milk, salt and spice, and melted butter. Add the flour and, last of all, currants and raisins, which have been sprinkled with flour. Steam two hours in a tin pail set in a kettle of water and serve hot with sauce.

Hasty Pudding

Into a dish of boiling water (a double boiler is best) stir Indian meal, very slowly. Let it cook for an hour. The water should be salted a little. Turn this into a bowl. The next day, or when perfectly cold, cut into slices and fry in pork fat or hot lard. This is served with molasses.

Baked Indian Pudding

2 Quarts of Milk 1 Cupful of Yellow Cornmeal 1 Cupful of Molasses 1 Teaspoonful of Salt

Put one quart of the milk into an earthen puddingpot, and the other quart of the milk into an agate dish, on the stove, to scald. Stir the meal into the hot milk slowly, one handful at a time, until it thickens. Remove from the stove and add molasses, pouring the mixture into the cold milk. Bake six hours in a slow oven; serve warm with cream. If properly cooked; it will be red and full of whey.

Orange Pudding

4 Oranges 3 Cupfuls of Milk 1 Cupful of Sugar 3 Eggs 2 Tablespoonfuls of Cornstarch Pinch of Salt

Remove peel and seeds from the fruit and cut fine. Sprinkle over the oranges half the sugar. Let stand for a few hours. Beat the yolks of the eggs, add the rest of the sugar, cornstarch and salt, and stir into the boiling milk. Pour this, when cooled, over the oranges and sugar. Beat the whites of the eggs to a stiff froth and add two tablespoonfuls of sugar. Spread this over the top and brown in the oven. To be eaten cold.

Plum Pudding

Take ten or twelve Boston crackers, split them open and soak over night in milk. Use a large pudding dish that will hold three or four quarts. Put in a layer of crackers, a handful of raisins, two tablespoonfuls of sugar, cinnamon and nutmeg, and a little butter on the crackers; repeat this three times. Have a layer of crackers on the top. Make a custard of three or four eggs, five is better, one cupful of sugar, a little salt, and milk enough to fill the dish within two inches of the top. Bake in a slow oven four or five hours. Let stand until cold, and it will slip out whole. Serve with hot sauce.

Queen's Pudding

1 Pint of Bread 1 Quart of Milk 3 Eggs 1 Cupful of Sugar 1 Teaspoonful of Butter 1 Lemon

Soak one pint of bread in a quart of milk till soft. Beat together the yolks of the eggs, sugar, butter, and the juice and rind of half a lemon. Stir all together and bake until it rises, about an hour and a half. When nearly cold, spread the top with jelly, and then the white of the eggs, beaten stiff. Brown in the oven. To be eaten cold.

Poor Man's Rice Pudding

1 Quart of Milk 1 Small Cupful of Sugar 1/2 Cupful of Washed Rice (scant) 1 Piece of Butter, size of a Hickory Nut 1/2 Teaspoonful of Salt 1 Teaspoonful of Vanilla

Bake slowly for three hours; the success lies in the baking. If baked right it will be creamy on top.

Suet Pudding

1 Cupful of Molasses 1 Cupful of Milk 1 Cupful of Chopped Suet 1 Cupful of Raisins 3 Cupfuls of Flour 1 Teaspoonful of Nutmeg 1 Teaspoonful of Soda 1 Teaspoonful of Salt 1 Teaspoonful of Clove 1 Teaspoonful of Cinnamon

Beat the soda into the molasses, add milk, salt and spices. Cover the raisins and suet with some of the flour, stir all together. Steam three hours in a tin pail, set in a kettle of boiling water. Serve hot with cold sauce, made of one cupful of sugar and one-third cupful of butter, creamed together. Grate a little nutmeg over the top.

Tapioca Cream

1 Quart of Milk 5 Tablespoonfuls of Tapioca 3 Eggs 1 Teaspoonful of Corn-starch 2/3 Cupful of Sugar Pinch of Salt

Soak the tapioca in a little warm water for an hour. Put the milk on the stove in a sauce pan. Add the sugar and salt to the beaten yolks of the eggs. When the milk is scalded put in the soaked tapioca and when boiling, stir in the eggs. Cook a few minutes and remove from fire. Stir in the beaten whites and flavor. To be eaten cold.

SAUCES

Chocolate Sauce

1 Tablespoonful of Butter 2 Tablespoonfuls of Cocoa 1 Cupful of Sugar 4 Tablespoonfuls of Boiling Water

Put the butter into an agate dish on the stove; when melted, stir in the cocoa and sugar dry; add boiling water and stir until smooth. Add vanilla to taste.

Cold Sauce

Cream together one-half cupful of butter and one and one-half cupfuls of sugar. Grate a little nutmeg over the top.

Cranberry Sauce

Pick over and wash one quart of cranberries; cover with cold water and cook until tender. Remove from the fire, rub through a colander and sweeten to taste.

Cream Mustard

1/2 Cupful of Vinegar 1/2 Cupful of Sweet Cream 1 Egg 1 Teaspoonful of Salt 1 Tablespoonful of Mustard

Put the vinegar on the stove and let it come to a boil. Have the cream, salt, mustard, and egg well beaten together, and pour the boiling vinegar over them, then set the whole over boiling water and stir constantly until it thickens. When cold, it is ready for use, and is very nice.

Egg Sauce, for Chocolate Pudding

2 Cupfuls of Sugar 1 Egg 1 Cupful of Boiling Milk Flavoring

Beat the egg and sugar together, and pour over it the boiling milk, and flavor.

Pudding Sauce

1 Cupful of Sugar 1/2 Cupful of Butter 1 Pint of Water 3 Heaping Teaspoonfuls of Cornstarch Flavoring

Cream together the butter and sugar. Wet the cornstarch with a little water; stir it into the pint of boiling water and, when thickened, pour it over the butter and sugar. Add the flavoring.

Salad Dressing

1/2 Cupful of Vinegar 1/2 Cupful of Water 1/2 Cupful of Milk Piece of Butter size of a Walnut 1 Egg 2 Tablespoonfuls of Sugar 1 Tablespoonful of Flour 1 Tablespoonful of Mustard 1 Teaspoonful of Salt

Put the vinegar, water and butter on the stove, in an agate dish, to boil. Mix together sugar, flour, mustard and salt, stir into the beaten egg with the milk, and add to the boiling water and vinegar. Let boil until it thickens. This is quickly and easily made, very nice and always a success.

Sauce, for Graham Pudding

1 Cupful of Sugar 1/2 Cupful of Butter 1 Egg 1 Lemon 1/2 Pint Boiling Water

Cream together the butter and sugar, add the well-beaten yolk of egg, pour over this the boiling water, juice of lemon and well-beaten white of egg.

SOUPS

Bean Porridge

Pick over and wash two-thirds of a cupful of white beans.
Put on the back of the stove in cold water. Let these boil
slowly, while the dinner is cooking. When the boiled
dinner has been taken up, put these beans into the liquor in
which the dinner was cooked. Boil one hour. Wet three
tablespoonfuls of flour with water, and stir in while boiling,
to thicken. Serve hot, adding a little milk, if you like.

Connecticut Clam Chowder

3 or 4 Slices of Salt Pork 3 Potatoes 2/3 Onion 1 Cupful of
Tomatoes 3 Crackers 1 Teaspoonful of Parsley 25 Soft-
shelled Clams 1 Quart of Water Salt and Pepper 1 Cupful
of Milk

Cut three or four slices of salt pork and fry in the bottom of
a kettle. Add the potatoes cut into dice, onion shaved, a
cupful of stewed tomatoes, rolled ship crackers, minced
parsley, soft-shelled clams, and boiling water. Add salt and
pepper to taste and cook till the potatoes are tender. A little
hot milk may be added just before taking up.

Massachusetts Clam Chowder

3 Quarts of Clams 6 Medium-sized Potatoes 1 Small Onion
8 Boston Crackers 4 Slices of Salt Pork

Wash the clams clean, put them on the stove to cook, with one pint of cold water. Boil until the shells burst open. Remove from the stove, pour the clam liquor into an earthen dish and set away to settle. When the clams have cooled a little, pick them from the shells, remove the night-caps, cut off the head, to the shoulders, washing each clam. Cut three or four slices of fat salt pork and fry in the bottom of a kettle with half an onion. Skim these from the fat, pour in the clam liquor, add a little hot water. When this boils, add the raw potatoes, which have been pared and sliced thin, and cook until tender. Split the crackers open and soak till soft in milk or water. Add these and the clams to the potatoes. Cook ten minutes, then add a quart of milk and salt, if needed. Do not let it boil after adding the milk. Serve hot. This is very delicious.

New England Fish Chowder

4 Slices of Fat Salt Pork 6 or 8 Potatoes 1 Small Onion 2 or 3 Pounds of Fresh Haddock or Codfish 8 Boston Crackers

Fry the salt pork, with the onion, in the bottom of a kettle, skim from the fat, and pour in about a quart of water. Slice the potatoes thin, after they have been washed and pared. Make alternate layers of fish and potatoes, seasoning each layer with pepper and salt. Cook until both are tender. Then put in the split crackers, which have been soaked in milk or water, as for clam chowder. Cook for ten minutes. Pour in a quart of milk, add a small piece of butter and serve hot.

Lamb Broth

2 Pounds of Fore-Quarter of Lamb 2/3 Cupful of Rice 1
Tablespoonful of Salt 1 Teaspoonful of Sage Leaves

Put the lamb into a kettle, cover with cold water, add the
salt and cook three hours. As the water boils away, add
more. Wash the rice, allowing three-fourths of an hour to
cook; put in the sage, about fifteen minutes before serving,
and thicken with two tablespoonfuls of flour, wet in two-
thirds of a cupful of water. The sage may be left out if
preferred.

A Good Oyster Stew

25 Oysters 1 Teaspoonful of Flour 1 Quart of Milk Butter
Salt

Take twenty-five oysters, with their liquor and put these
into an agate dish on the stove with salt to taste, in a pint of
cold water. Boil five minutes. Stir into this one heaping
teaspoonful of flour, which has been wet with two
tablespoonfuls of cold water. Add one quart of milk. Let it
come to a boil, but be sure not to have it boil. Remove from
the fire, and add a piece of butter the size of an egg. This is
sufficient for eight people.

Potato Soup

4 Potatoes 3 Pints of Milk Piece of Butter size of an Egg
Small piece of Onion

Take four large potatoes, boil until done and mash smooth, adding butter and salt to taste. Heat the milk in a double boiler, cook the onion in it a few minutes and then remove. Pour the milk slowly on the potato, strain, heat and serve immediately. Thicken with one tablespoonful of flour.

VEGETABLES

Green Corn Fritters

2 Cupfuls of Corn, grated from the cob 2 Eggs A Little Salt
1/2 Cupful of Milk 1/2 Cupful of Flour 1 Level
Teaspoonful of Cream of Tartar 1/2 Level Teaspoonful of
Soda

Beat the eggs, then add the milk and salt. Stir the corn into
the dry flour, wetting with the milk and eggs, then fry in
hot lard.

Delicious Stuffed Baked Potatoes

Bake six potatoes, or enough for family. When done, set
away to cool slightly. Cut off a small piece, scoop out the
inside, mash, add butter, salt, and milk, also tiny bits of
parsley, if liked. Fill the shells with this mixture, put back
in the oven and bake until brown.

Creamed Potatoes

4 or 5 Baked Potatoes 1 Pint of Milk 1/2 Teaspoonful of
Salt Butter, the size of a Walnut

Pare the potatoes and cut into small pieces. Put them on the
stove, in an agate dish, salt and cover with milk. Let them
cook fifteen or twenty minutes, then thicken with one

tablespoonful of flour, stirred with half a cupful of water; put in the butter and serve hot.

Scalloped Potatoes

Butter a baking-dish, pare and slice potatoes in small pieces. Put into the dish with salt, pepper and a little butter. Fill the dish with milk, sprinkle over the top cracker or bread crumbs, and cheese, if you like it. Bake in the oven for an hour and a half or two hours.

Baked Tomatoes

6 Tomatoes

2 Cupfuls of Bread Crumbs

Small piece of Onion

A Few Stalks of Celery Hearts

Salt and Pepper to Taste

Cut off a small piece of each tomato and scoop out the inside. Mix this with two cupfuls, or the same amount of bread crumbs, the chopped onion, salt and pepper. Then fill the tomatoes with this mixture, putting small pieces of butter over the top. Place these in a pan in which is a very little water, to prevent sticking, and bake in a hot oven from twenty minutes to half an hour.

Fried Tomatoes

Pare and slice (not very thin), dip into flour and fry on a griddle in hot fat.

APPENDIX

HOUSEHOLD HINTS OLD AND NEW FOR HOUSEKEEPERS YOUNG AND OLD

To Save Confusion in the Home

"Plan your work, then work your plan."

Monday—Wash, if you have it done in the house. If sent out, use that day for picking up and putting things in order, after the disorder of Sunday.

Tuesday—Iron.

Wednesday—Finish ironing and bake; wash kitchen floor.

Thursday, Friday—Sweep and dust, thoroughly.

Saturday—Bake, and prepare in every way possible, for the following day.

Have in or Near Your Sink

A handle dish cloth.

A wire dish cloth.

A cake of scouring soap.

A small brush for cleaning vegetables.

These articles are indispensable. Also have two cloths, which must be kept perfectly clean.

One for washing dishes.

One for washing sink.

Homemade Shortening

Do not throw away small pieces of fat from pork, lamb or steak. Put them on the stove, in a skillet or agate dish and cook them till there is nothing left, but scraps. Then pare a potato, wash clean, cut into thin slices and cook in the fat for a half hour to clarify it. Strain through a cloth. This will be good to fry doughnuts in and for all purposes, where shortening is needed, except for pie crust.

Pieces of fat, not fit for shortening can be saved in some old utensil and made into kitchen soap.

To Make Tea and Coffee

Always use freshly boiled water. Do not boil more than three or four minutes. This is very important, in making a good cup of tea or coffee. Never use water which has stood in the teakettle over night.

A Use for Left-over Coffee

Do not throw away the coffee you have left from breakfast. If you do not care for iced coffee for dinner, make a little coffee jelly, by the recipe on page 27.

Never Throw away Old Underclothes

Keep them for housecleaning, for washing windows and for washing lamp chimneys. Old pieces of calico, or flannel make good holders to use about the stove. Wash, boil and dry cleaning cloths when soiled, that they may be ready for use again.

That Leaky Hot-Water Bag

Do not throw away an old hot-water bag because it leaks. Fasten over the leak, a strong piece of adhesive plaster. Fill the bag with sand or salt and cover with flannel. It will hold heat for a long time, and can be used instead of the water bottle.

To Keep your Hands White

Keep a piece of lemon in your bathroom or kitchen. It will remove stains from the hands.

To Brown Flour

Spread flour upon a tin pie plate, put it in a hot oven, and stir constantly, after it begins to brown, until it is all colored. Keep always on hand. It is good for coloring and thickening gravies.

Lemons and Fish

Lemon juice makes a very grateful addition to all kinds of fish. Thin slices of lemon, with sprigs of parsley, around a platter of fish, makes a pretty garnish.

To Try out Lard

If you want good sweet lard, buy from your butcher, leaf lard. Skin carefully, cut into small pieces and put it into a kettle or sauce pan. Pour in a half-cupful of water, to prevent burning, and cook slowly, until there is nothing left but scraps. Remove the scraps with a skimmer, salt it a little, and strain through a clean cloth, into tin pails. Be sure not to scorch it.

How to Keep Eggs

In the summer, when eggs are cheap, buy a sufficient
number of freshly laid ones to last through the winter.

Take one part of liquid glass, and nine parts of cold water
which has been boiled, and mix thoroughly.

Put the eggs into a stone crock, and pour over them this
mixture, having it come an inch above the eggs. The eggs
will keep six months, if they are perfectly fresh when
packed and will have no taste, as when put into lime water.

Save your Old Stockings

Old stockings are fine for cleaning the range. Slip your
hand into the foot and rub hard, or place an old whisk
broom inside. It will make the sides and front of the range
clean and shiny. In fact, you will seldom need to use
blacking on these parts.

When Washing Lamp Chimneys

If you live in the country and use kerosene lamps, do not
dread washing the chimneys. Make a good hot suds, then
wash them in this, with a clean cloth kept for that purpose.
Pour over them very hot or boiling water and dry with an
old soft cloth. Twist a piece of brown paper or newspaper,
into cornucopia shape and place over the chimneys to
protect from dust and flies.

To Remove Disagreeable Odors from the House

Sprinkle fresh ground coffee, on a shovel of hot coals, or burn sugar on the shovel. This is an old-fashioned disinfectant, still good.

To Lengthen the Life of a Broom

Your broom will last much longer and be made tough and pliable, by dipping for a minute or two, in a pail of boiling suds, once a week. A carpet will wear longer if swept with a broom treated in this way. Leave your broom bottom side up, or hang it.

To Prevent Mold on Top of Glasses of Jelly

Melt paraffine and pour over the jelly after it is cold. No brandy, paper, or other covering is necessary.

To Clean Nickel Stove Trimmings

Rub with kerosene and whiting, and polish with a dry cloth.

To Clean Zinc or Copper

Wash with soap suds and powdered bristol brick. When perfectly dry, take a flannel cloth and dry powdered bristol or any good cleaning powder and polish. You will be pleased with the result. I have tried this for forty years.

How to Prevent Button Holes from Fraying

When making button holes in serge or any material which frays, place a piece of lawn of two thicknesses, underneath and work through this.

Another way is to make four stitchings in the goods the length of the button hole. Cut between these, leaving two stitchings each side of the hole.

When Making a Silk Waist

Stitch a crescent shaped piece of the same material as your waist under the arm. It will wear longer and when the outside wears out it looks neater than a patch. If the waist is lined, put this between the lining and the outside.

To Make Old Velvet Look New

Turn hot flatirons bottom side up. Rest these on two pieces of wood, or hold in your lap. Put over them a piece of wet cloth, then lay the velvet on this. Brush with a whisk broom. The steam from the wet cloth will raise the nap and take out the creases.

Onion Skins as a Dye

If you wish for a bright yellow, save your onion skins. They will color white cloth a very bright yellow. This is a good color for braided rugs, such as people used to make.

To Remove Egg Stain from Silver

Salt when applied dry, with a soft piece of flannel will remove the stain from silver, caused by eggs.

Put a Little Cornstarch in Salt Shakers

This will prevent the salt from becoming too moist to shake out.

How to Color Lace Ecru

If you wish for ecru lace and you have only a piece of white, dip it into cold tea or coffee, until you have the desired color.

To Keep Lettuce Crisp

Put it into a paper bag and place right on the ice. It will keep a week in this way.

To Keep Celery

Do not put it into water. Wrap it in a cloth, wet in cold water and place directly on the ice.

To Keep a Piece of Salt Pork Sweet

Put it in a strong brine made of one quart of cold water, and two-thirds of a cup of salt.

Save Potato-Water

Pare potatoes before boiling, and then save the water, to mix your yeast bread with.

A Use for the Vinegar Off Pickles

When your pickles have been used from your glass jars, do not throw away the vinegar. Use it in your salad dressing. It is much better than plain vinegar because of the flavor.

Do not Allow a Child to Eat Fresh Snow

This often looks clean and pure but fill a tumbler with it, cover to keep out the dust and then show it to the child, that he may see for himself, the dirt it contains.

When Making Hermits or Cookies

Instead of rolling and cutting as usual, drop the dough into a large iron pan. The heat of the oven melts them into one sheet. Cut them into squares or long narrow strips. It takes much less time, than the old way of rolling and cutting.

To Clean a Vinegar Cruet on the Inside

Put into it shot, pebblestones, or beans. Fill it with a strong soap suds, and one teaspoonful of bread soda or ammonia. Let stand an hour, shake well and often. Rinse with clean water.

To Make Tough Meat, or a Fowl Tender

Put one tablespoonful of vinegar, into the kettle while boiling.

To Remove Black Grease

Rub patiently with ether. It will not leave a ring, like gasolene, and will remove every trace of the stain.

To Keep an Iron Sink from Rusting

Wash with hot suds. When dry rub it well, with a cloth wet with kerosene. Do this three or four times a week and your sink will look well, all the time.

How to Add Salt to Hot Milk

Salt will curdle new milk, so when making gravies, or puddings, put your salt into the flour, or with eggs and sugar, to add when the milk boils. Use a double boiler for milk gravies and gruels.

To Soften Boots and Shoes

Rub them with kerosene. Shoes will last longer, if rubbed over with drippings from roast lamb. Old-fashioned people always used mutton tallow on children's shoes.

A Way to Cook Chops

Pork or lamb chops are very nice, if baked in a hot oven. Turn them as they brown. It saves the smoke in the room.

When Cooking Canned Corn

Place it in a double boiler to prevent scorching.

Salted Almonds

Shell the nuts and put into boiling water. When they have stood for fifteen or twenty minutes, the skin will slip off easily. When dry, mix a half-teaspoonful of olive oil or butter, and a quarter of a teaspoonful of salt, with a cupful of nut meats. Spread on a tin pan, and place in a hot oven. Bake fifteen or twenty minutes. Watch closely and stir several times, as they burn quickly. Treat peanuts in the same way.

Before Washing Colored Clothes

It is wise to set the color first, by soaking in a strong solution of cold salt water (one cupful of salt to half a pail of water). Soak two hours.

To Remove Iron Rust from White Goods

The old-fashioned way, still good, is to wet the place in lemon juice, sprinkle on it common table salt, and lay it in the sun. In these later days, there is on the market an iron rust soap, which removes the spot quickly, also an ink eradicator, sold by all druggists.

How to Make Starch

Two tablespoonfuls of starch should be made into a smooth paste with four tablespoonfuls of cold water. Pour over this three pints of boiling water, stirring rapidly all the time. Starch the garments, while they are still wet. In the olden days, people made starch of flour in the same way, for linen and gingham dresses, as it was less expensive and thought to be just as good for colored clothes.

When you Go Away from Home for a Few Days

Plan your meals before leaving. This simplifies matters for the one left in charge, and is often found to be of importance financially.

The Proper Way to Sweep a Room

Dust the furniture and put it in another room. Dust bric-a-brac and put on the bed if you are sweeping a sleeping room, if another room put them on the table, or in an adjoining room. Brush the draperies, take down and lay on the bed or table. Cover these and bric-a-brac with a sheet. Wet a newspaper, tear into small pieces and spread on the rug or carpet. Now you are ready for sweeping. If the floor is carpeted, sweep all dirt to the center of the room. Sweep the corners with a small whisk broom. Move every piece of furniture lest there be dirt left underneath. Open the windows before sweeping. When the dust is settled take a pail of warm water, put in a tablespoonful of ammonia, then with a clean cloth wrung from this wipe the window glass, mirror and pictures; polish with dry cloth. Wipe all finger marks from doors and mop boards.

Now take a pail of clean water, with ammonia, and with a small scrubbing brush go over the rug or carpet, to remove dust and brighten the colors. Replace furniture, bric-a-brac and draperies and your room will be sweet and clean. With care, once in two or three weeks, will be often enough to do this.

When Baking Cup Custards

Set them into a pan of hot water. When you remove from the oven, place them in a pan of cold water, to prevent longer cooking.

When Using Currants and Raisins

Mix a little dry flour with currants and raisins before adding them to cakes or puddings. It will keep them from falling to the bottom.

Try Baking Beets, Instead of Boiling Them

They are much sweeter. Three or four hours is necessary, according to size.

When Making Grape Juice or Jelly

Before adding the sugar, strain through a flannel bag. It will be much clearer.

When Sewing Braid on a Dress

Slip a piece of pasteboard three or four inches long, into the hem. You can sew more quickly, and your stitches will not show on the right side.

To Skin Beets

When you remove beets from the kettle, plunge them into a dish of cold water. The skins will slip off easily with the hand. Never cut or pare beets before cooking.

A Fine Way to Keep Cut Roses

Immerse them at night in a pail of cold water, blossoms down.

To Keep Carnations

Put a little salt in the water, which should be changed each morning, and cut the stems a little each time.

When Pies are Ready to Bake

Put little dabs of lard, on the top crust, then hold it under the faucet, letting cold water run over it.

A Way to Make Pies Brown and Shiny

Just before putting a pie in the oven, brush over the top with milk, using a soft brush or a clean piece of cheese cloth.

When Threading a Needle

Place a piece of white paper under the eye. You will be surprised at the ease, with which you can thread it.

Make your Own Baking Powder

Get your grocer to weigh for you one pound of cream of tartar, and one-half pound of bread soda. Sift these together nine times in a flour sifter. Put in a tin can, and it is ready for use.

To Prevent Children from Losing Mittens

Sew strongly to each mitten, four or five inches of narrow black ribbon (use a colored one if you prefer). Sew the other end of ribbon to the coat sleeve. The child can remove mittens at any time without losing them and always know where they are.

Teach a Child to Hang up his Own Coat and Hat

Have some hooks, low down in the closet or kitchen where a child can reach them easily, to be used only by himself.

To Keep your Own Umbrella

Take a piece of narrow white tape, three or four inches long. With a glass pen, or a new clean steel one, and indelible ink, write your name upon it. Sew this to the inside of the umbrella.

To Wash a White Silk Waist, or a Baby's Bonnet

Use cold water and white soap. Hot water will turn white silk yellow.

When Ironing Embroidery

Place it right side down on a piece of soft flannel, ironing on the wrong side. If flannel is not at hand, try an old turkish towel.

To Wash Small Pieces of Lace

Put in a horse radish bottle and pour over them, strong soap suds, good and hot, and shake well. Let stand awhile and shake again. Rinse in clear, warm water, by shaking. Dry on a clean cloth in the sunshine.

Never Throw away Sour Milk

It is excellent for graham bread, gingerbread, brown bread, griddle cakes, and doughnuts, also biscuit.

You can make a delicious cottage cheese of a very small quantity.

Set the milk on the back of the stove, in an agate dish. Let stand until the whey separates from the curd. Strain through a cloth, squeezing the curd dry. Put in a little salt, a small piece of butter, and a little sage if desired. Press into balls and serve.

Mark New Rubbers

Take a pointed stick—a wooden skewer from the butcher's is best—dip it into ink and write the name, on the inside.

Economical Hints

Save small pieces of soap in the bathroom, by placing in a cup or small box, until you have a cupful. Add a little water and boil a few minutes; when nearly cool, press with the hands, and you have a new cake of soap.

Do not throw away the white papers around cracker boxes. They are good to clean irons and will save buying ironing wax. If irons are dirty put a good layer of salt on newspaper and rub the irons back and forth.

Save even the coupons on your soap wrappers. You can get a silver thimble for your mending bag with them, if nothing more.

Save your strong string, to wrap around packages going by parcel post. Also fold nicely for further use your clean wrapping papers. Make a bag of pretty cretonne, hang in the kitchen or cellar way, to keep the string and wrapping paper in. You will find it very convenient.

Do not throw away small pieces of bread. Save them for plum pudding, queen's pudding, or dressing for fish or fowl. If broken into small pieces and browned in a hot oven, it is very nice to eat with soups. Or, dry well, roll fine and keep in a glass jar, to be used for breaded pork chops, croquettes, or oysters.

To Mend Broken China

Stir into a strong solution of gum arabic, plaster of Paris. Put this on each side of the china, holding together for a few minutes. Make it as thick as cream.

To Clean Old Jewelry

Wash in warm water containing a little ammonia. If very dirty rub with a brush. This is very good also for cleaning hair brushes and combs.

Dish Washing Made a Pleasure

First of all, remove all refuse from the dishes. Place them near the sink, large plates at the bottom, then the smaller ones, then saucers. Have a large pan full of very hot water. Make a good soap suds by using a soap shaker. Wash the tumblers and all glassware first, and wipe at once. Use a handle dish cloth (which can be bought for five cents), for these, as the water will be too hot for the hands.

Wash the silver next. Have a large pan, in which to place the clean dishes, cups and bowls first. When all are washed pour over them boiling or very hot water, and wipe quickly. Pans and kettles come last. Always have a cake of sand soap or a can of cleaning powder, for scouring the pie plates and bottoms of kettles. It is very little work to keep baking tins and kitchen utensils in good condition, if washed perfectly clean each time they are used.

Wash the dish towels, at least once every day, and never use them for anything else. With clean hot water, clean towels, and plenty of soap dishwashing is made easy.

If you live in New England, your sink will be in front of a window. Be sure and plant just outside of this window nasturtiums, a bed of pansies, morning glories and for fall flowers, salvia. These bright blossoms will add to your pleasure while washing dishes.

A Space Saver

If you are crowded for space in closet, kitchen or pantry buy a spiral spring, such as is used for sash curtains. Fasten the end pieces to the back of the door, and stretch the spring from end to end. You now have a fine place to hang towels, stockings or neckties, or if used in a pantry, to keep covers.

Another Space Saver

If you have no closet in your room, get a board, nine inches wide, and three or four feet long. Put it in the most convenient place in your room on two brackets. Stain it the color of your woodwork. Screw into the under side of the board, wardrobe hooks. Now get a pretty piece of cretonne or denim, hem top and bottom, and tack with brass headed tacks to the shelf, having it long enough to come to the floor, and around the ends of the board. Use the top for a book shelf or hats.

If the Freshness of Eggs is Doubtful

Break each one separately into a cup, before mixing together. Yolks and whites beaten separately, make a cake much lighter than when beaten together.

When Bread Cooks Too Quickly

When your bread is browning on the outside, before it is cooked inside, put a clean piece of brown paper over it. This will prevent scorching.

To Remove the Odor of Onions

Fill with cold water kettles and sauce pans in which they have been cooked adding a tablespoonful of bread soda and the same of ammonia. Let stand on the stove until it boils. Then wash in hot suds and rinse well. A pudding or bean pot, treated in this way, will wash easily. Wood ashes in the water will have the same effect.

Never Leave a Glass of Water or Medicine, Uncovered in a Room

This is very important. Water will absorb all the gases, with which a room is filled from the respiration of those sleeping in the room.

Weights and Measures

4 Teaspoonsfuls equal 1 tablespoonful of liquid.

4 Tablespoonfuls equal half a gill.

2 Coffee-cupfuls equal 1 pint.

2 Pints equal 1 quart.

4 Coffee-cupfuls of sifted flour equal 1 pound.

1 Quart of unsifted flour equals 1 pound.

1 Pint of granulated sugar equals 1 pound.

1 Coffee-cupful of cold butter pressed down equals 1 pound.

An ordinary tumbler holds the same as a coffee cup.

It is well to have a tin or glass cup, marked in thirds or quarters for measuring.

When to Salt Vegetables

Every kind of food and all kinds of vegetables need a little salt when cooking. Do not wait until the vegetables are done. Salt the water they are boiled in after they begin to boil.

What to Serve With Meats

Roast Beef and Turkey

Squash, turnips, onions and cranberry sauce.

Roast Pork

Spinach, onions and apple sauce.

Roast Lamb

Mint sauce.

Roast Mutton

Currant jelly and vegetables.

With all kinds of meat and fowl pickles are always good.
Make your own pickles, after recipes found in this book.

The Length of Time to Cook Meats

Lamb

Roast a leg of lamb three hours. Wash clean, sprinkle over
it a little flour and salt and put into a pan, with cold water.
While it is cooking, take a spoon and pour over it the water
from the pan, three or four times.

Veal

Roast veal three hours, treating it the same way as lamb. When you have removed it from the pan, make a smooth paste, by wetting two or three tablespoonfuls of flour with cold water, and stir into the water left in the pan. Pour in more water, if the size of your family requires it.

Beef

Roast beef requires fifteen minutes for each pound. Do not salt beef, until you take it from the oven.

Ham

Boil a ham of ordinary size three hours. Let cool in the water in which it is boiled. It is very nice to remove the skin, while warm, stick cloves in the outside, sprinkle over it a little vinegar and sugar and bake for one hour.

Sausages

Sausages are very nice, baked in a hot oven twenty minutes. Prick with a fork to prevent bursting. Do this too, if fried.

Corned Beef

Should boil four hours.

Chicken

A chicken will cook in one hour and a half. A fowl requires an hour longer. Don't forget to put in one tablespoonful of vinegar to make tender.

Turkey

A ten pound turkey needs to cook three hours, in a slow oven.

The Length of Time to Cook Vegetables

Onions

Boil one hour. Longer if they are large.

Cabbage

Requires one hour and a half.

Parsnips

Boil two or three hours according to size.

Carrots

Wash, scrape, and boil one hour.

When Paring Tomatoes

Put them into very hot water and the skin will come off easily.

Made in the USA
Middletown, DE
08 September 2019